GIOVANNI GABRIELI

Oxford Studies of Composers

Oxford Studies of Composers (12)

GIOVANNI GABRIELI

DENIS ARNOLD

London
OXFORD UNIVERSITY PRESS
NEW YORK   TORONTO
1974

Oxford University Press, Ely House, London, W.1

GLASGOW NEW YORK TORONTO MELBOURNE WELLINGTON
CAPE TOWN IBADAN NAIROBI DAR ES SALAAM LUSAKA ADDIS ABABA
DELHI BOMBAY CALCUTTA MADRAS KARACHI LAHORE DACCA
KUALA LUMPUR SINGAPORE HONG KONG TOKYO

ISBN 0 19 315231 2

© Oxford University Press 1974

*Printed in Great Britain by
W & J Mackay Limited, Chatham*

CONTENTS

PREFACE

THIS short study is an offshoot of a larger one. It has been written to provide an introduction to an important composer for the reader who wishes to avoid the detailed analyses which a more ample monograph must necessarily contain. If it presents a picture somewhat different from that usually painted, it is simply because it is based on a closer examination of the Venetian setting in which Gabrieli worked. The classic study of his life and times, Karl von Winterfeld's *Johannes Gabrieli und sein Zeitalter*, was published nearly a century and a half ago. Winterfeld was one of the great scholars of his day whose notebooks, still preserved in a German library, reveal that he looked at an incredible amount of sixteenth- and seventeenth-century music. His command of the period was such that his study will never be superseded, the more especially as he wrote in a clear style which any subsequent musical scholar must envy. His picture of Gabrieli was limited only by the fact that one man could not hope to transcribe more than a fraction of the music which surrounded his subject. Much of this is now available in modern editions. Thus where Winterfeld inevitably saw Gabrieli against only the major figures of the time, such as Palestrina, today there is a wealth of background material, both musical and documentary, with which to fill in the portrait.

Winterfeld naturally stressed the political nature of Gabrieli's work, that it was a glorification of the Venetian Republic, in contrast to the devotional attitude of the Roman school as exemplified by Palestrina. He was aware that this was not the sole quality of Gabrieli's music—his chapter on the later works is masterly—but, perhaps because he was a civil servant, he was fascinated by this aspect, as have been later writers. And it is not to be denied that the Venetians were the greatest practitioners of this kind of art, both in painting and sound. But when Giovanni Gabrieli's music is set against that of his predecessors Claudio Merulo and his uncle Andrea, his colleagues Giovanni Croce and Giovanni Bassano, and his pupils, in particular Heinrich Schütz, a more sophisticated musician begins to appear. There are various significant facts to be taken into account. He was apparently a less fluent composer than his masters and colleagues, for though some of his music has certainly been lost we have only to compare his somewhat restricted range with that of his many-sided uncle to see the difference. In mood, a comparison with Croce's church music makes plain

Gabrieli's greater concern for depth and his profound religious conviction. Finally, the fact that he has bequeathed to us a substantial corpus of instrumental music, while his Venetian colleagues have left very little indeed, shows an interest in the abstract uncharacteristic of a purely, or even mainly, political composer.

These considerations may change our attitude to both listening and performing his music. He is no brash composer, to be played loudly on brass instruments. He has a Venetian grandeur, it is true, but it is tempered by a Counter-Reformation intensity which may give his late works a closer relationship to such contemporary music as Monteverdi's *Vespers* than merely the outward appearances of spatial effects and large forces. Most of all, Gabrieli emerges with a distinct personality, rather than as a national monument. Like Purcell and Elgar, to mention two English composers who had a similar role and have had similar reputations, his public music is of lesser importance than that which expresses his individuality; and since he wrote for an audience, as well as for himself, it is not difficult for us to find him sympathetic, even in an age when both processional glory and nationalism are no longer fashionable.

THE EARLIEST YEARS

WE do not know the date of Giovanni Gabrieli's birth, but the available information, not altogether to be trusted, suggests that it was about 1555, or perhaps a year or two later. He was a native Venetian, and Venice was then at a peak of glory. Not that this glory was a matter of military might; the Most Serene Republic had lost battles in the past and would lose more in the future. But it had arranged its affairs so that its inhabitants had a sense of political security which is worth more than the prowess of arms. If the hindsight of historians has proclaimed that with the new trade routes to America, Venice was already in decline, a merest glance at the chaos of a Germany torn by religious strife, or still more at the England of the 1550s, comprehensively uncertain of what the immediate future might hold (for no one could then predict what the courage and cunning of a long-living Maiden Queen would do), shows why Venice was envied throughout Europe. The reign of its elected Doges protected it against the perils of inherited succession, its geographical isolation made it secure against the depredations of most armies, its skill at diplomacy meant that its wars were fought from afar. It was a highly desirable place in which to be born.

For a musician it was especially so. At the time of Gabrieli's birth, Venice was undoubtedly one of the great centres of music making. It had not always been. At the beginning of the century, the courts of the Estensi and the Grand Dukes of Tuscany had been more active in attracting those famous Netherlanders to whom Italian music was to owe so much. The names of the Venetians Francesco d'Ana or Giovanni Fossa cannot compare with those of Josquin or Obrecht. Venice entered the lists late, when Willaert was made *maestro di cappella* at St. Mark's in 1528. But once this had happened, the stability of Venice made tradition take a firm hold. Willaert's pupils were many and various, and by the 1550s Venice was full of good musicians, players, singers, and composers. Only Rome could, perhaps, compete with it in sheer numbers, and even Rome was less interesting, simply because Venice was not only a place where one could hear great music in its churches, but was full of secular music-making of all kinds. A host of madrigal books appeared from the Venetian presses of Scotto and Gardano, inspiring local composers to satisfy the world's demands for good music for domestic performance. Venetian music of this era is astonishing for its variety as much as its quantity. Grand motets and psalm settings, instrumental pieces for ensemble or keyboard, witty villanelle and serious Petrarchan madrigals, all are grist to the Venetian mill. The Serenissima was in mid-century one of the most exciting cities in which a composer could grow up.

Which of these musicians Giovanni Gabrieli knew must be largely a matter of speculation. Willaert died too soon to have been the young man's teacher; which may have been just as well, for Willaert was by then quite old, and, in the event, Giovanni obtained a notable mentor who perforce was more in touch with the latest fashions. Giovanni's uncle, Andrea Gabrieli, was still an unknown when his nephew was born, an organist at a not particularly famous parish church, S. Geremia, and a contributor to one or two minor anthologies of madrigals. Though one cannot be certain of even the decade when he was born, Andrea seems to have been no eager youngster in 1555, but a man well in his thirties. This makes his future career all the more surprising: fifteen years later, he was not only organist of St. Mark's; he was one of the best known of all Venetian composers. This sudden rise can only be accounted for by one event. In the early 1560s Andrea went to Munich, presumably to work at the Bavarian court. It was a journey which brought him into touch with a wealthy patron possessing a large musical establishment such as even a Doge might envy. It brought him into touch with some future patrons. More than that, it brought him some musician friends of great worth, and especially the most famous of all European composers, Orlando di Lasso.

When Andrea was in Munich, Lasso was seemingly a gay person, capable of taking an active part in a court comedy, certainly capable of writing bawdy French or German songs which would have shocked some of his Roman contemporaries. His versatility was amazing. There is scarcely any kind of music which he had not mastered. Masses, motets, madrigals flowed from his fluent pen, and in a myriad different styles. His travels, like those of Mozart two centuries later, had made him the complete cosmopolitan, and to a man like Andrea Gabrieli, born and bred in a single city, his example must have been most invigorating, Andrea, who returned home to be appointed to one of the best posts open to a musician in Venice, seems to have done his best to emulate him. Admittedly there are no chansons or polyphonic lieder: but everything else soon appears. The masses and motets, the *giustiniane* which are a Venetian equivalent of the chanson or villanella, the madrigals, sometimes elegant, more often light and very singable, the *canzoni alla francese* for keyboard, the ricercars for instrumental ensemble, the grand madrigals in praise of a visiting prince exploring the delights of Venice—there is scarcely a genre with which Andrea did not become fully familiar. There is scarcely another Italian composer so prolific, so universal—or thus it seems on the surface. Probe a little deeper, and Andrea is not quite as close to Lasso as might appear. For one thing, he lacks the sharpness of wit, that Netherlandish gift for the realistic vignette, which often can be found in Lasso's chansons. For another, he is more extrovert, less sombre than Lasso sometimes is, even in the 1550s and 1560s (and Lasso became more serious as life went on). He is a public composer rather than a devotee of the intellectual, inward-looking *musica reservata* of the Munich circle. Emotionally, the elder Gabrieli is less complex than Lasso, though perhaps as fine a musician.

This was probably as well for his pupils, of whom there were many. And we may be certain that his nephew was one of them. Giovanni was very fond of his uncle. 'If Messer Andrea Gabrieli (of blessed memory) had not been my uncle, I would dare to say (without fear of seeming biased) that, as there are few illustrious painters and sculptors together in the world [at any one time], so there have been very few such excellent composers and organists as he was. But since by ties of blood I am to him little less than a son, it is not fitting for me to say freely about him that which affection directed by the truth might suggest to me . . .' he was to write in the dedication of the famous volume of *Concerti* which was the memorial prepared by the nephew to honour his uncle a year after Andrea's death. These are not conventional words even in the circumstances. Giovanni's esteem for his uncle glows in many a work, and though their temperaments were not identical, the similarities between certain madrigals and motets by the two unmistakably point to a pupil-teacher relationship. What did Andrea's teaching consist of? A revealing anecdote by another pupil gives us a hint.

Among the many pupils (among which number I also was) that Sig. Andrea Gabrieli, most honoured organist of St. Mark's, possessed, there was one whom I will not name who had made many counterpoints upon a *canto fermo*, and being tired of it, asked the master whether he could change it; and, the master looking at him with displeasure, he said 'Please, Master, let me change this *canto fermo*, for I do not know what more I can do with it', and taking up a pen, he [Gabrieli] composed four or five *fughe*, the one more beautiful than the other, and said 'Do you really think you had done everything possible . . .'[1]

Andrea clearly believed in technique—and then more technique. In

[1] L. Zacconi, *Prattica di Musica*, Cap. 33, p. 83.

this anecdote there is no suggestion of the Renaissance philosophizing of his colleague, Zarlino, whose own teaching of counterpoint is leavened by other considerations, such as methods of combining words and music, and whether the ancient Greeks meant this or that. The down-to-earth attitude here reported may well account for certain qualities of sheer musicianship which Giovanni shows in an era when they were not universally popular. It certainly accounts for the superbly dexterous polyphony which informs so much of his most splendid music.

Andrea's handing on of traditional ways was not confined to his own teaching. It must surely have been as the result of his advice that his nephew is next heard of in Munich. Giovanni was indeed working there when the earliest of his music to be printed came out in 1575. These two madrigals show that once again Lasso is acting as a catalyst on a Gabrieli. One of them is a setting of Petrarch's sonnet 'Voi ch'ascoltate', in a competent polyphonic vein, with due, but not excessive, attention to word-painting. It is a piece such as Lasso himself might have written—though not at the height of his inspiration, for it has little in the way of memorable ideas or flashes of insight into Petrarch's meaning such as Lasso shows in his *Primo libro de madrigali à 5 voci*, full of the most exquisite settings of that poet. Gabrieli's other madrigal is nearer to Lasso in both mood and mastery. 'Quando io ero giovinetto' is a splendid Netherlandish woodcut of the old man who was once one of the boys on the piazza. His *joie de vivre* has gone—and worse still, his attractiveness to the girls has gone too. No one wants to know him nowadays and he returns home quite sadly. Here the music adds a great deal to the verse. Triple time expresses the joys of youth, the sadness of age suggests discords, and even contrapuntal learning has its place when the *seconda parte* of the madrigal (the picture of age) inverts the theme used at the opening of the *prima parte* (the vision of carefree youth). The lively rhythms, the bright modern colours of the two sopranos in the ensemble help to make this a madrigal worthy of a much more mature composer. For a lad in his teens, it shows achievement as well as promise.

Giovanni stayed in Munich for some years. In 1578, he was seemingly a full member of the household, receiving both salary and livery from the Duke of Bavaria. It must indeed have been the experience of a lifetime. The musical establishment of the court was at its height—bigger than it had been in Andrea's day, though it had been ample enough then. It was an international group with Italians, Netherlanders, and Germans all contributing to its variety. Several of these excellent musicians were to turn up in Venice later in life, probably because of their friendship with Giovanni; and it was not just musicians who formed his acquaintances in Bavaria. He was obviously admired by a vast range of the musical upper classes, for most of his patrons, the people who sent him pupils or perhaps awarded him a present on the dedication of some music to them, were to be Germans. His reputation was made in Southern Germany, and he was more popular there than in any Italian state to the end of his life.

We do not know why or when he left Munich. His patron, Duke Albrecht, died in 1579 leaving a mountain of debts which his successor Wilhelm felt bound to discharge. Wilhelm was a lover of the arts; he was also one of the princes who can be said to have taken an active part in the Counter-Reformation, introducing the Jesuits to Bavaria to combat incipient Protestantism. The gaiety of his father's court was reduced in the 1580s, as the grand comedies with musical intermezzi gave way to religious dramas acted by the boys of the court chapel. Even Lasso was affected by the new atmosphere, and his last years were clouded by a religious melancholia that saddened his wife and friends. So it is possible that the younger Gabrieli left with a number of other musicians in the early 1580s. He may have embarked on more travels, but his most likely occupation for these years seems to be that of organist at some minor Venetian church—there were well over a hundred and our knowledge today of their musicians is virtually non-existent. In any case, when we hear of him next in 1584, he is acting as temporary organist of St. Mark's, while the post vacated by the famous virtuoso organist, Claudio Merulo, recently departed for his native state of Parma, was advertised and filled. Andrea had clearly engineered this temporary employment with an eye to the future. His nephew formally applied for the job, was the best qualified of the candidates, and, after the usual tests in front of the board of State Procurators, he was given a post which he was to grace for over twenty-five years.

THE ORGANIST

THE two organists of St. Mark's were, to all intents and purposes, civil servants. As members of the Doge's *cappella*, they were given renewable contracts, with a fair amount of security, and a decent though not generous salary. The distinction of Andrea Gabrieli and Merulo had helped to give the posts a status which organists could not easily have found elsewhere. It was for these reasons that the Procurators took trouble in making their appointments, and had evolved a procedure for the competition between the applicants. The tests which each candidate had to take were, interestingly enough, tests of musicianship rather than of virtuosity, and they reveal what was expected of an organist in the later sixteenth century. They were, in effect, concerned with two arts, score reading and improvisation. In the first, organists were expected to be able to play from the four parts of a choirbook, so as to accompany a choir. In the second, it was considered important for them to take a plainsong theme and make a real piece of music from it, using it as a *canto fermo*, as the composition pupils of Andrea were made to do on paper. Both qualities were very necessary for keyboard players, since together with one other art—that of embellishment—they formed the basis of keyboard music. For the astonishing thing about organ music in late sixteenth-century Italy is how little original work had been printed. Doubtless some circulated in manuscript, and much has disappeared. The fact remains that, compared with the dozens of volumes containing motets or madrigals, printed keyboard music was a comparative rarity. Which meant the organist had to compose or arrange his own. The nature of the tests at the competition also underlines the role of the player in St. Mark's. Instead of having the opportunity to display his skill to an admiring audience, his main function was to provide a modest background at various parts of Mass and Vespers. On the grand festivals, pompous instrumental music was, as we shall see, the prerogative of what may fairly be called an orchestra. The organist, in all probability, came into his own on ferial days, when the choir sang a simple polyphonic setting of the Mass or Vesper psalms —and when, it must be said, there was no important array of Senate and Doge in the nave. This somewhat inferior function is underlined by the two instruments provided for the organists to play. By the standards of Northern Italy, the bigger of them was quite large:[1]

Sub-Principal Bass	24′	
Principal	16′	
Octave	8′	
Decimanona	3′	(a quint)
Quintadecima	3′	(a superoctave)
Vicesimaseconda	2′	(an octave biscomposita)
Vicesimasesta	1½′	(a quintlein)
Vicesimanona	1′	(octavatens composita)
Flauto	8′	

[1] Johann Mattheson, *Der Vollkommene Capellmeister* (Hamburg, 1739; reprint Kassel and Basel, 1954), p. 466.

There are difficulties in the interpretation of this specification, but clearly by the standards of Northern Europe this was no more than a miniature. If we look, for example, at the specifications of the splendid instruments on which Sweelinck played[2] it is not difficult to sense the relative importance assigned to organists in Venice and in the Netherlands.

Nonetheless, the Venetians did delight in the prowess of their organists, and the two salaried players at St. Mark's during Giovanni Gabrieli's early years were not only admirable performers: they also provided their profession with a substantial repertoire. Andrea Gabrieli and Merulo were obviously very different in their talents. The former's contrapuntal skill, his classical, extrovert approach to composition contrast with what can only be called a romantic flair, an appreciation of fantasy, in the latter. Their best organ music lies in opposing fields. Andrea is the master of the 'transcription' forms, that is, those which are derived closely from vocal models. His favoured source was the French chanson which had considerable virtues for his purpose. Its four-voiced texture often fitted under the fingers remarkably well, two voices for each hand. The French language sets to music in more regular metrical patterns than Italian, and thus the chanson is crisper in rhythm than the madrigal, an advantage to the keyboard player. The narrative quality rather than concentration on emotive words meant that there was a less rigid relationship between poem and music in the chanson—a *sine qua non* when you are about to remove the poem completely. And finally, the chanson often had a distinct musical shape, with a recapitulation of opening material at its end. When music must stand on its own feet rather than rely on the words to give it form, such a built-in resource was invaluable. Add the general tunefulness, of the Parisian composers more especially, and Andrea's penchant for chanson settings and imitations is very understandable. Many a mass must have been enlivened by his ear-tickling canzonas, which an irreverent singer might have whistled on his way out of St. Mark's.

If Andrea's canzonas are very much listener's music, his essays in the other 'transcription' form, the ricercar, are less so. The genre was rapidly becoming a display of learning which was what the term was to imply in the later seventeenth century. In place of the crispness of the canzona rhythms are the long white notes, the imitative counterpoint, and the lengthy overlapping phrases of the motet. But whereas the motet, by the second half of the sixteenth century, has an interest in sonority,

[2] A. Curtis, *Sweelinck's Keyboard Music* (Leiden and London, 1969), Appendix I, p. 163ff.

which leavens the polyphony with a variety of textures, the ricercar concentrates on the working out of themes in a frankly didactic manner. They are often enough teaching pieces—teaching playing or composition—and are meant for private pleasure rather than public display. Andrea, as a master of counterpoint, clearly enjoyed the purity of the ricercar, unbeholden to words or indeed to anything except the whim of his musicality and skill. Though it must be said that even here cheerfulness will keep breaking in. The distinction between canzona and ricercar is frequently blurred by Andrea's extroversion. He entitles some pieces 'ricercari ariosi' and these are indeed airy rather than searching, tuneful rather than learned.

All these works stick to the main outlines of vocal models quite strictly and could indeed be quickly converted to music for use by an ensemble. Their organistic quality is to be found only in one respect: there are many embellishments of the melodic lines. The art of ornamentation was taught as the art of filling in gaps. Each interval could be decorated by a series of figures worked out so as not to obscure the harmony too much, while giving the chance of great variety. The instrumentalist seeing an upward moving fifth in a melodic strand could, if he liked the methods of Giovanni Bassano of St. Mark's orchestra, add the following adornments:

Even a narrow interval such as a descending third need not lack one of these flourishes:

There is an *embarras de richesse* in the number of ornaments invented by such ingenious virtuosi. The musician's art comes in their selection and usage. The elder Gabrieli, it may well be, was not very concerned with the display of dexterity, and he uses *fioritura* to underline the structure of his polyphony rather than to show his skill. When he applies ornaments to his ricercars, they remain an embellishment rather than an essential. The opening bars of his 'Ricercar al nono tono' would sound well if the trills and twirls were removed.

Ex. 3

a) Simplified version

b) Original

This is where Merulo had something to teach Giovanni Gabrieli. He was interested in the effects by which ornamentation can alter the whole conception of a piece. He was clearly a great improviser; and this is an art which demands the ability not so much of the long-range thinking which is Andrea's métier, as of accepting the suggestion of the moment and making the most of it. For Merulo, an ornament was just such material. Out of a double mordent he can create a whole toccata, introducing it casually in apparently conventional polyphony or allowing it to take charge in passages where display is the main feature. From embellishment comes also a more sophisticated harmony, for the very nature of ornaments is to be dissonant—not always violently, but nonetheless significantly discordant if used *en masse*. And it is Merulo's great gift to see that when there is much encrustation, the separate strands of polyphony cannot be appreciated as such by the ear, which will follow the ornaments rather than the continuous flow of melody. Thus strict part-writing is largely irrelevant. It is the total effect which matters, and some of the rules of counterpoint, for example those concerning the 'preparation' of suspensions, are, for the organist, not particularly important. The freedom of resolution of discords, for which Monteverdi was so hotly attacked in those heady years of revolution around the turn of the century, can be found earlier in Merulo's organ work. It is not difficult to appreciate that he was Frescobaldi's teacher, for they show the same romanticism, the same gift to let the player's whim take over, to give free rein to pure creativity.

Merulo taught Giovanni Gabrieli much less than he did Frescobaldi: they were not temperamentally akin. Like his uncle, Giovanni was not a great writer of virtuoso toccatas. Of his dozen or so essays in this genre which have survived, most are frankly rather dull. The passage work sprawls, as though the fingers are mechanically applying the semiquaver scales advocated for the less inventive by the treatises. Left hand will imitate the right hand; there may be, as in the Sixth Toccata, more elaborate polyphony at times; and, like Bach in his sonatas for solo violin or cello, Gabrieli can suggest counterpoint by splitting a phrase into segments in different registers, so that the illusion of two strands is created. But these are far from the imaginative strokes of Merulo. There are two exceptions, and significantly they occur in a single manuscript source which could mean they are late works (there are stylistic traits[3] which support this conclusion). The Ninth and Tenth Toccatas[3] both show a Merulo-esque capacity to use embellishments in an interesting way. The Ninth begins with a bouncing dotted rhythm which involves some irregularly treated passing notes, and when the fingers begin to show their suppleness, the passage work quite often involves the superimposition of one chord on another, as the logic of the ornament goes in opposition to the held chords of the other hand. The Tenth is an even more exciting piece, its ornaments again more full of character—though it is typical of Gabrieli that its splendid beginning is notable for its counterpoint, and its sombre sonorities.

Ex. 4

[3] *Numeration as in the collected edition, ed. S. Dalla Libera (Ricordi)*

If Merulo's flights of fancy have only a small place in the younger Gabrieli's music, his uncle's extroversion finds not much more room in it either. Perhaps it was the fact that, by the 1580s, French chansons were less popular than they had been in Andrea's youth, which caused the complete disappearance of that kind of transcription from Giovanni's *oeuvre*; one cannot help thinking that neither was it much to his taste. The only transcriptions we do find under his name in the sources are of some of his grandest motets—and we cannot be sure that he made them himself. Be this as it may, these arrangements do show why the organists of Giovanni's mature years were having to turn to writing original music for their instruments: these grand motets just will not reduce satisfactorily for keyboard. Without the variety of colour and texture of the originals, they lose all their essential character. An organ transcription is no more than an aid to knowledge, as is a piano duet version of a Beethoven symphony. Where, on the other hand, Gabrieli adopts the manner rather than the letter of the transcription in his canzonas, he shows himself a master. All the half-dozen works in this genre could well have been originally written for an ensemble, and some are certainly re-workings of ensemble music. In a sense, they are not therefore strictly organ music; which does not mean that they do not sound extraordinarily well in this form. That they are offshoots of Andrea's canzona style is self-evident; but they are on the whole more sophisticated, both in technique and emotion. The first canzona in the Foa manuscript at Turin, for example, begins in Andrea's bluff major-key, crisply rhythmic, contrapuntal way, with ornaments only to mark the ends of sections, and with the contrasts between paired 'voices' derived from the old Netherlandish style. What is original is the emotional expansion at a great climax near the end, where a simple repetition of an idea is suddenly extended, and then is further developed by an exploration of new tonalities.

Ex. 5

The quickening of intensity by the dissonances in this passage, albeit nothing that breaks any of the 'rules', shows how the younger Gabrieli can change a mood; and the second canzona of this collection equally makes it clear that, for him, the simple tunefulness of his uncle is rarely enough. It is a skilfully wrought piece, apparently in the major (as the first chord to contain a third suggests), and it is seemingly a rondo, a form popular in Venice, with a gay triple-time refrain. In fact, it is neither major in mood, nor a simple rondo in form. The major third nearly always sounds as though it is part of a dominant on its way to a tonic—and that tonic is virtually always minor. As for the refrain, it is never twice the same, and it has to be provided with several transitions to install it in the main body of the piece. The expectations aroused by jaunty rhythms, the appearance of gaiety, are almost always belied.

These canzonas are interesting music, which might be expected, since the genre was the most popular of instrumental forms by Giovanni's mature years. It is more surprising to find that his best organ music comes in his ricercars and fugues, the scholarly pieces which testify to his worth as a teacher. And scholarly they certainly are. In the eighty bars of one of them, only the final flourish cannot be directly related to the theme with which it opens; the more than sixty bars of another have only two bars displaying new material—and since the main theme includes a scale as a principal feature, even these can be said to have been derived from the subject without much stretching of the imagination. Yet such pieces do not sound in the least academic. Part of the secret comes from the nature of Gabrieli's fugue subjects. Like Andrea's, they frequently begin with chanson rhythms which bring an immediate feeling of impetus. They are also usually quite big, indeed beginning that tradition of extended subjects which lasts in Italy to the time of Vivaldi, offering the composer a great deal of material to develop. In the second so-called 'fuga' of the Giordano manuscript in Turin, the ingredients seem made for a lengthy discussion. The canzona motif repeating the dominant will provide an ideal way of establishing a tonality: the sequential keyboard figuration which follows is excellently designed for creating mounting excitement; while the downward scale which brings up the rear is a useful link which will accompany chordal pomp at the climax. The result is a splendid piece, varied in emotion, the more especially since the harmonies are rarely predictable, for major and minor can be closely juxtaposed and the long opening notes of the subject are fully utilized as pedal notes, building tensions on assumed dominants as surely as a nineteenth-century composer. Moreover, it has the feel of genuine keyboard music, for the *fioritura* has been well integrated into the melodic patterns; and if there is a fairly strict adherence to four quasi-vocal polyphonic strands, it is noticeable that the consistent use of the bright upper notes of the Venetian organ would be impossible on most other instruments (and all voices) of the time: the uppermost line would tax the lips and breath of even the virtuoso cornettists of the St. Mark's orchestra. In fact, most of these ricercars have that sense of flair in exploiting both sonorities and material which will be apparent in Gabrieli's grander music.

The restrictions of a small instrument, with seemingly few advantages, can also be a stimulus. There is a great deal of the quintessential Giovanni in this modest output of organ music. He was not a virtuoso as was Merulo, nor a provider of cheerful tunes as was his uncle. He was a learned musician, a true craftsman who enjoyed manipulating notes. More than that, he is a composer whose technical subtlety allows him to explore the pastel shades of emotion. In the best of both canzonas and ricercars there is an ebb and flow of feeling, a capacity to change moods hardly—and yet sufficiently—perceptibly. Thus these underperformed works are a convenient starting point for considering his more famous works in which these virtues are of the utmost importance.

THE MADRIGALIST

FAME was acquired, then as now, away from the organ loft. For composers of the last twenty-five years of the sixteenth century, it was madrigals that made their fortunes, since it was these which sold well, or, by means of a suitable dedication, might be rewarded by a gift from a noble patron. It was a madrigal which was the most widely reprinted and diffused of Gabrieli's works—and though 'Se cantano gli augelli' is indeed a splendid piece, it can hardly compare in emotional vitality and sophistication with many of his greatest motets and instrumental works. There are three dozen of his secular vocal pieces which have survived, not by any means an insubstantial corpus until, perhaps, it is set against the fecundity of his uncle or his colleague Giovanni Croce. It is the way these works appeared which gives us reason to believe that he was a reluctant madrigalist. There is not a single complete collection dedicated to his secular music, not even a major section of one of his grand volumes of *Concerti* (significantly these are called *Sacrae Symphoniae*) devoted to it. Virtually all of it appeared in single numbers as part of an anthology, compiled by someone else; or, as in the case of the half-dozen madrigals included in a posthumous collection of his uncle's music, as a makeweight when a publisher might want a volume to be less slim. It seems almost as though a direct commission was necessary to make him put pen to paper in this genre. He is the very opposite, in this respect, of Marenzio or his master Lasso.

The nature of the madrigals confirms this view. Nearly a third of them are not written for a few voices to give domestic pleasure, but are in effect (and sometimes clearly so marked) choral pieces, with or without instrumental support. They are in the truest sense *al fresco* works, meant for performance on occasions when some nobleman, one of the Augsburg Fuggers, perhaps, was giving a grand entertainment, or was being entertained by official Venice. One work, 'O che felice giorno', we can trace to a performance of a rather bad pastoral play given in front of the Doge in the courtyard of the Palazzo Ducale. Several other madrigals which do not demand such resources set verse which implies performance at a wedding or some similar celebration. Giovanni seems to be the successor of his uncle in this sphere too, for it was Andrea who wrote the music for the public merrymaking when Venice went mad with joy after the victory at Lepanto and decorated floats filled with singers and players were paraded round the Piazza S. Marco. Though the documents do not enable us to know exactly when Giovanni's grand secular pieces were given, it is fairly certain that they were composed in not dissimilar circumstances.

Some of the bigger pieces were included by the publisher Gardano in a volume called *Dialoghi*. This might suggest that Giovanni's approach to the problem of writing grand secular music was essentially

dramatic, and he has been considered a precursor of the opera composers of the turn of the century. It is true that 'O che felice giorno', as
the finale of the anonymous pastoral, was probably performed in an
arrangement which allowed a couple of solo voices, accompanied by
lutes, to sing the upper lines of Giovanni's twin choirs, before the rest
of the singers joined in; and the piece is peculiarly tuneful (when later
turned into a motet by a German anthologist it sounds strangely
irreligious). But dramatic is scarcely the word for it, for there is none of
the drawing of character which that term usually implies. There is
somewhat more of this aspect in another dialogue, 'Dolce nemica mia',
which he included among Andrea's *Concerti* in 1587. This is in a well-
worn Venetian tradition, for composers often concluded a madrigal
book with a semi-dramatic scena, usually an explicit expression of the
lovemaking of Thyrsis and Chloris, or Phyllis and Damon, those
Arcadian shepherds and shepherdesses whose flirtations were the very
stuff of the madrigal in the 1580s and 1590s. Giovanni, like his colleagues
Baldassare Donato and Giovanni Croce (and, for that matter, Thomas
Morley, who imitated Croce in a detailed fashion in one of his madrigal
books), paints the lovers in a rough and ready way by using upper voices
for the girl, lower voices for the boy; though rough and ready it
certainly is, since a voice from either group can reinforce the other if a
fuller texture is required. There is more psychological insight in the
actual musical material: the shepherd's growing animation from slow
'white' notes to the quicker crotchets and quavers, as he is provoked by
the girl's flirtatious, villanella-like cross-rhythms and the fragmentary,
questioning motifs with which she displays her charms. But any real emotion is saved until the end, when with all seven voices at his disposal,
Gabrieli finds inspiration in the voluptuous dissonances such forces offer.

Ex. 6

23

This final tutti offers the key to Gabrieli's approach to the grand madrigal. He is not really interested in conveying the trivial emotions of those idealized rustics so much as creating a noble sonority to please the assembled company. Thus his dialogues are in reality secular motets, an art which he had probably learned from Lasso, who wrote some splendid works in this vein to honour his Bavarian duke. Certainly the mighty piece in honour of the Fuggers, 'Sacri di Giove augei', with its dexterous lively counterpoint in twelve very real parts, is in Lasso's manner, and with the voices supported by the Munich ensemble (for it might date from Gabrieli's years there) would have sounded very well. Two other pieces maybe dating from the same era are no less effective, though both 'Chiar'angioletta' and 'Lieto godea' are neither motets nor madrigals, but *canzone francesi*, written on the largest possible scale. 'Per cantar et sonar', they are marked; and from them we again see Gabrieli's taste for abstract music. The rhythms of the music are essentially French in their orderly accentuation, even though the Italian verse might suggest a freer approach. Then there is the same recapitulation of material without any need for it in a madrigalian idiom, suggesting the Parisian composers of decades earlier. If the pieces were played rather than sung, they could still have much to offer. 'Lieto godea' especially became popular in its day, being provided with a German text by one enterprising Transalpine publisher, and also being used as the basis of a parody mass by that admirer of the Gabrielis, Adriano Banchieri. This is not difficult to understand, since it has that fascinating bitter-sweet quality that one finds so often in Giovanni's music, coming from the instability of the major-minor relationship which informs the piece from the opening bars.

None of the smaller works which Gabrieli contributed to the anthologies is quite so plainly in the French style, but the canzona is often in their hinterland. A great proportion of them begin with the motto rhythm ♩ ♩ ♩, and many of them use repetitions of various kinds to give a sense of shape. Sometimes it is no more than a traditional re-statement of an opening or closing section but, as in his organ works, there are likely to be differences in the working out, as in 'Da quei begl'occhi', where a new ending is provided to a phrase, or in 'S'al discoprir', where the difference between the two final sections amounts to a full re-working. It is not uncommon, either, for motifs throughout a madrigal to be related to one another in rhythm, and in 'Da quei begl'occhi' one feels that, as in a keyboard ricercar, one idea is constantly suggesting another. It is this flair for construction that makes Gabrieli a master of the canzonetta, an unlikely genre for such a serious man, but in the event one in which it is a shame that he indulged so infrequently. The three he contributed to his pupil Francesco Stivori's *Vaghi e dilettevoli madrigali a quatro voci* are all quite charming, never greatly emotional (which would be beyond the scope of the genre) but full of art, tuneful without having a monotonous regularity of phrase, simple in harmony but not without flashes of imagination whereby a chromatic progression can suddenly add a new dimension. (See Ex. 8.)

It is this talent for making pure music which helps to define his position as a madrigalist in the 1580s, when most of these works were written. It was a decade dominated by Marenzio, the genius of an art wherein music and words are combined in a close way, towards which composers had been aspiring for thirty years. It is an art in which the

Ex. 8

Ahi, senza te

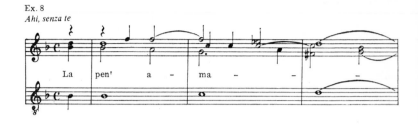

La pen' a - ma - - -

- - ra, Deh, di - mi do - ve sei.

poetry contributes concrete images which the composer can interpret in emotional terms. It is to some extent a slightly trivial art, for deeper feelings are rare in it, the pastoral convention decreeing a sophistication which is foreign to the *grand amour*, or to quasi-religious devotion. It was a highly attractive art to those willing to accept this convention, for it mirrored the artifice of court life, and its virtuosity of thought and manners, while never making too strenuous demands on an amateur's musicality. Which is precisely where Gabrieli refuses to fit in. He accepts the convention as far as it provides him with musical resources. He likes the bright colours of the Marenzian style, with its use of the female voices to brilliant effect (though he knew something of this from his uncle). He likes also the simplicity of idiom, which allows splendidly singable melody and clear-cut diatonic harmonies. He even adopts at times the more flexible approach to word-setting of Italian, where the constant joining together of syllables or their elisions makes for a fluidity unknown to the Netherlanders brought up (musically speaking) on French or Latin. But from the basic philosophy he stands aloof. When, for example, he contributed a madrigal to a collection called *La Ruzina*, he set a poem in which a modern composer would surely have revelled. 'If I have wounded you, I have not caused your death': this is promising stuff, full of the *double entendre* of the Marenzian 'poesia per musica'. Or is it? When Gabrieli puts it to music, the answer would seem to be 'no'. To actually refuse the passion of dissonance—nay, the ordinary cadential suspension—for the word 'death', must be very rare in 1591. The most he will do is take a passing note slightly irregularly.

26

Ex. 9

S'io t'ho ferito

non t'ho   pe - rò,   mor - to

Perhaps the most immediate way of realizing his basic stance is to put one of his madrigals alongside one by Marenzio; and since both contributed to *Il Trionfo di Dori*, it can be done quite fairly, as both were writing for the same occasion, the celebration of the wedding of a Venetian nobleman. The verse is the usual pastoral nonsense, and Gabrieli accepts the convention for once: the animals gambol with a playful motif, Cupid's arrows are shot in canonic imitation, the fish in deep water are seen through the descending scale. It is only when 'Se cantano gli augelli' is compared with Marenzio's 'Leggiadre Ninfa' that we realize how essentially musical Gabrieli is. Black notation for shady valleys, a turn for 'fior', triple time for the dancing satyrs; Marenzio never has time for the solid musical development of the Venetian. And when both come to the refrain 'Viva la bella Dori', how quickly Marenzio despatches it: Gabrieli more than doubles his ten bars in a glowing coda of firm counterpoint which inevitably reminds an Englishman of the equal glories of Weelkes' 'As Vesta was from Latmos Hill descending', from a volume of 'Triumphs' in the sincerest flattery of the Italian. (See Ex. 10.)

The comparison with the Englishman is not fortuitous: the two have much in common. Gabrieli, like most of the English madrigalists, was an organist and a craftsman, not one of the image-makers of the late madrigal. Like Morley or Wilbye, he is no longer interested in the genre when it involves the over-sophistication of the avant-garde, of Monteverdi, Gesualdo, and the rest of the mannerists. Like theirs, his music is most enjoyable to sing, and it is a pity that the attention given to his church music has seemingly precluded the wider diffusion of his madrigals and canzonets, which are an amateur's delight. Though, it must be said, his farewell to the secular is unique to Venice. The last madrigal we possess is in a manuscript at Kassel, preserved most probably by Heinrich Schütz. It is a vast dialogue for vast forces, which the words suggest was meant for a *favola marittima* given to welcome the new century in 1600. These forces are divided into two groups, one of Sirens, the other of Tritons. As ever, the dramatic aspects of the dialogue are weak; the grand sound is overwhelming. The cornett demanded in one of the partbooks is just one of the great array of voices and instruments which surely gave its audience a feeling of power and security that day. Its climax seems to convey that sense of continuity so beloved of the Serenissima. Venice, already older than any other civilized state, could look forward to a new century with its customary almost arrogant confidence.

Ex. 10

FESTIVALS AT ST. MARK'S

THE music for which Gabrieli is best known is that which he wrote for the grand ceremonies at St. Mark's. It was probably the force of circumstances which made him compose in this vein, rather than a preference for it. The organists of the basilica were not always composers of this type of music: Andrea's immediate predecessors and Giovanni's immediate successor were not particularly involved in it, and then it was left to the *maestri* in charge to produce motets and vesper psalms. But when Giovanni was appointed to his post, Zarlino was still *maestro di cappella*, and he was a theorist and theologian rather than an active composer. So the custom which had grown up in about twenty years for the organists to be the principal composers of festival music was continued, and when Andrea died in 1586, the mantle inevitably descended on his nephew. Whether he found this role to his taste we shall never know, but it may be significant that when his prolific colleague, Giovanni Croce, became first *vice-maestro*, and then the Director of Music, Gabrieli's output seems to have gone down. Only some three dozen motets survive which can probably be dated from the last fifteen years of his life; and by no means all of these are works in the grand manner. Be that as it may, St. Mark's was fortunate to have him in these years, and we are fortunate that his duties impelled him to the mastery of the glorious Venetian style.

For it was a time of glory in Venice. The Battle of Lepanto had been the Venetians' finest hour—or so it seemed. From the 1570s until 1605, there was no holding back their sense of splendour. The chroniclers of this era can scarcely contain their sense of pride, and as the State celebrated the events of its past, or entertained a royal visitor, or as a Doge rejoiced in his election, it was done with due, indeed excessive, pomp. The Doge during Gabrieli's central years at St. Mark's, Marino Grimani, was one of the most splendid figures of the time, spending so much money on both alms and feasting at his election in 1595 that one wonders how he had still more to pay for the coronation ceremony of his wife (a totally superfluous ceremony of dubious meaning and no antiquity) a couple of years later. It is hard for the modern sophisticate, for whom ceremony has largely lost its symbolic significance and for whom patriotism is not nearly enough, to understand the sense of holiday and festival of the sixteenth-century citizen. In the great processions, a large part of the populace was involved, as the men from the confraternities, the religious of the various orders, joined with the nobility of Senate and Grand Council in moving around the Square. The actual sequence of events on such days was laid down by precedent, preserved carefully in great books of descriptions compiled by the master of ceremonies in St. Mark's (they are now in the Venetian State Archives). The place of each group of men, from the Doge to the humblest priest or guild officer, was thus ordained, not always quite the same for each festival but appointed to suit the occasion. And Venice being what it was, to omit an observance on a traditional festival day amounted almost to a major political decision. So year after year these high days were observed by the Signory, the laity, and the priesthood. 'It is our custom to accompany the religious with the temporal', wrote one commentator, explaining the constitution of the processions. It is the most succinct statement of the situation, which helps to explain the nature of the grand paintings of Gentile Bellini or Tintoretto, the grand motets of the Gabrielis.

For the composer, these festivals must have been at once a burden and an inspiration. The burden came from the nature of his task which was to produce settings of texts of limited emotional range. The Venetians rarely set the Ordinary of the Mass. The two settings by Giovanni Gabrieli to survive complete, the half-dozen by Andrea, and the handful of large-scale settings by Giovanni Croce, when compared with the dozens by Palestrina and Lasso, underline the fact that Venice was not particularly interested in the significance of that sacrament. This is important, since the separate parts of the Ordinary give a composer an incomparable emotional range. This the Venetians had to seek in the psalms for Vespers, which they often did compose. But those for the grand occasions of state generally speak of rejoicing, and this is automatically a restriction. Their most fruitful liturgical text was perhaps the Magnificat, which most of the St. Mark's school set many times. Apart from this, there were the prayers for the days appropriate to Venetian saints—St. Mark, St. John the Baptist—and for Venetian circumstances, either because of some relic preserved in St. Mark's, such as the Holy Blood and the Cross, or because of some historical accident, such as St. Marina's Day, whose festival happened to coincide with the anniversary of the return of Padua to the Republic in 1512. There were also the greater festivals of the Church year: Christmas, Epiphany, Easter, Ascension (turned into an almost exclusively state occasion by the wedding of the sea ceremonies), and the various days devoted to the Blessed Virgin, for whom Venetians felt a special affection. There was a certain amount of variety in the prayers for these days, but there is no doubt that often the motet texts do not readily suggest the subtler shades of emotion or even the strong contrasts that can be found in a wider cross-section of the feasts of the year.

The compensation for the composer must have lain in the fact that he could assemble almost limitless forces to perform his music. 'Almost limitless' is, of course, a comparative term: the limits are those of the imagination, and composers of this time could hardly summon up in the mind the numbers of musicians involved in, say, the Berlioz *Te Deum* or Mahler's *Symphony of a Thousand*. Nonetheless, most sixteenth-century composers would have been content with the forces hired by the Procurators on these occasions. The actual choir at St. Mark's was not particularly large. At a low ebb in the 1590s it consisted of only two sopranos, four altos, three tenors, and four basses; more normally it probably numbered about thirty, which was the total membership of a proposed guild of its singers in the early years of the seventeenth century. The instrumental ensemble was proportionately larger, half-a-dozen salaried players being supplemented at will by fifteen or twenty free-lance *stromentisti*. These were versatile enough to provide a composer with any combination of sounds he might require, though most were wind players. Among both singers and players were splendid virtuosi. The soprano singers were castrati, often brought from Spain or the Spanish dominions in Southern Italy; the cornettists and trombonists were of the highest calibre, and in Giovanni Gabrieli's day often men who had had experience in Munich and elsewhere. With the brilliance of the two organists, to whom sometimes a third player on a portable instrument was added, the total effect was often enough marvellous, as the accounts of many a foreigner tell us. 'La musique est fort bonne' said the Frenchman Du Val; 'delicate and rare' are the words of Thomas Coryat. So it was.

To dispose these grand forces to the greatest effect, the Venetians had evolved the art called 'cori spezzati', or separated choirs. Since a single choir loft at St. Mark's would hardly take the total number of musicians with ease, they were split between the two galleries on either side of the altar. It sounds as though this might present difficulties of ensemble, but in fact, these galleries are not so very much farther apart than the choir stalls of a large un-Byzantine church, and the musicians in one are plainly visible to those in the other. When more sophisticated spatial effects were required, matters became more complicated, since a group of singers might be put on the floor of the church—but even then they were kept within the choir, and not disposed in the nave or the more distant galleries (the vogue for really dazzling *spezzato* gimmickry in the seventeenth century was largely the work of the imitators of the Venetians in Bologna, Rome, and Southern Germany).

The style which emerged from these arrangements was derived from the ancient mode of antiphonal psalm singing, whereby each choir would sing a verse in turn, both choirs joining in for the doxology. But such simple antiphony did not survive for long, since the temptations to exploit the contrasts inherent in this manner were too strong. Although the development of the style has not yet been investigated in detail, it is clear enough that it was in Andrea Gabrieli's lifetime that *cori spezzati* emerged as a formalized medium, and that Andrea himself was one of its most cunning exponents. Andrea probably learned the elements from Willaert, whose *Di Adriano et di Jachet: I salmi appertinenti alli vesperi . . . a duoi chori* have some claims to have set off the vogue, and from Lasso, who used the multichoral manner for grand motets in praise of his monarch. Andrea's perception was to combine traits evident in both. From Willaert he learned the virtues of simplicity, both in harmony and texture; from Lasso he learned that sophistication need not be completely abandoned, and that the sheer magnificence of sound is enhanced when counterpoint is not neglected. To which he added an extraordinary appreciation of sonority. In the works of his last years (as far as we can date them) he realized that making each 'choir' have a tone colour of its own, using the distinct sound quality of various types of instrument, can give a new interest to the music. At the doxology of his *Gloria* for four choirs, perhaps written

Ex. 11

in 1585 for the visit of some oriental princes, we see the essence of his style. The harmony is simple, but the counterpoint is excellently skilled; the sheer range of sound is acquired by differentiating each choir quite clearly, while using the vast range given to the lowest note of (probably) trombones and the highest notes of (probably) cornetts. The effect is literally astonishing.

Andrea is the master of this kind of grandeur and his nephew learned a great deal from him. Giovanni's first published compositions using *cori spezzati* include a Christmas motet, 'Angelus ad pastores', which might well be the work of Andrea. Twelve voices in two choirs, one of high, the other of low tessitura, proclaim their message. The harmony is simple, relying on the dominant-tonic relationships which Andrea also liked. The texture is simple also, and though counterpoint is not neglected, the chord-changes at regular intervals emphasize the strong accentuation which gives the piece its impetus. The range from top soprano to bottom bass is fully exploited, implying instruments even where they are not strictly necessary. The individuality of the separate strands has been compromised by this desire for an overall effect, but the words are clear in the predominant homophony. It is Venice at a post-Lepanto Christmas.

Ex. 12

This mood and manner is to be found in many of the works of the *Sacrae Symphoniae* of 1597. The Easter motet 'Surrexit pastor bonus'

is in the same vein, and it is noticeable that once the initial ideas have been introduced by the separate choirs, the tutti is involved for nearly all the work, giving a splendour of sound which certainly outdoes the more modest settings by such people as Palestrina and Lasso. St. Mark's Day is another suitable occasion for the grand double choir and 'Virtute magna' is given a similar treatment, though here one can detect a greater subtlety, for the material is developed more fully, the single choirs are allowed longer phrases, and the climax comes with a series of closely worked canons. This must have been extremely difficult to perform accurately in St. Mark's, where the resonance would confuse the exact timing necessary, but it is not impossible, since the basic melodic material is regularly shaped. Gabrieli gains an astonishing fullness by this rigorous counterpoint, in which no half beat is ever without its accent in one or another parts, and the pursuit of one voice by its fellow in the other choir gallery is relentless.

Such command of polyphony is commonplace in Giovanni's grandest

Ex. 13

music, and though in some of his later music octave doubling becomes normal enough to suggest that he was feeling the desire to simplify, the grand climaxes of a motet for sixteen voices, such as 'Omnes gentes', or one for nineteen, such as 'Buccinate', will show the same dexterity in the manipulation of independent parts. It is largely a matter of rhythm, rather than pure melody, on this scale. The repeated note given life by syncopation is the stuff of it, a trick learned from Lasso, perhaps, certainly a favourite of Andrea, and this might seem to make it fake rather than genuine polyphony. But true polyphony is a contrasting of rhythms as much as of separate melodic growth, and thematic development of the sort common in the Netherlandish style would be totally inappropriate for these resources. This working out of succinct, simple rhythmic formulae is the only method of keeping motets and masses to reasonable dimensions, and it helps to account for the excitement of the Gabrielis' music, in particular of Giovanni's, as opposed to the poise of the Roman style.

It means also that the shaping of the music has to be done another way; and to the organist used to the canzona the most obvious method was by repeating sections with or without variations. This was not unknown in motets throughout the sixteenth century, since the liturgy frequently uses refrains or *alternatim* practice whereby priest and people answer one another. This comes in handy in such a piece as the 'Hodie Christus natus est' setting for ten voices. The *cori spezzati* are given contrasting tessituras, and typically for Giovanni it is the lower choir, the *coro grave* as it was often called, which takes the burden of the argument, singing the text of the motet complete, in solemn sonorities, mainly homophonic in texture but bursting with animated syncopated counterpoint at moments of excitement. This is broken up by allelujas in which the tutti is deployed, the same music being used no less than six times. And how this refrain dances in its triple time, with that cross-accent so typical of the composer!

Ex. 14

36

The climax, it must be supposed, comes at the Andrea-like statement of the doxology, where both choirs state the proposition in chords laid out over more than three octaves; but it is noticeable that it is the refrain which brings the piece to a close, considerations of musical shape determining the whole, not the pattern of the text. This happens quite often in Giovanni's motets, as in the exquisite and economical setting of 'Regina caeli' (of which Merulo made a similarly splendid rondo), and the gorgeous 'Plaudite' for three choirs. Even where there is no possibility of a repetitive structure, it is noteworthy that the abstraction of the alleluja is attractive to him. Over a quarter of the grand 'Maria virgo' is taken up with the alleluja, no less than two-fifths of 'Deus qui beatum Marcum'; and it is remarkable that while some of these sections seem stripped down to a stereotyped rejoicing, there are others which are quite subtle. That of 'Maria virgo' in particular is no formula, with the dancing rhythm of the example above (Example 14) superimposed on duple time, to a great confusion of accentuation, while the answering phrases firmly restate the main beats of the bar, to make it clear that this is meant to be heavily syncopated music. In fact, the delight of many of these grandest works comes in such refrains where the composer's imagination is stimulated by the purely musical potential.

That it was also stimulated by the instrumental resources of St. Mark's on these festival days is shown in the number of times Giovanni divides his 'choir' into three or even four groups rather than the two of the motets already discussed. Not that colour is a minor part in their magnificence; it is at the heart of their being. Yet it is when Gabrieli feels he must make further divisions that we can see how this aspect of the Venetian style is suggesting new ways. His motets and a number of his Magnificats are often disposed for three groups, each having a different sonority. One of these may be a *coro grave*, four strands of which the uppermost is usually written in the tenor clef, the lowest in the 'double bass' (i.e. with the F on the top line); another may be a *coro superiore*, the uppermost part in the treble clef, the lowest usually in the tenor; and the third choir is frequently a straightforward soprano-alto-tenor-bass group, being sometimes marked *cappella*. There are words under each part in the sources, but to try to give a purely vocal performance is to court disaster. In any case, from a compendium of Italian ways expounded by Michael Praetorius to enlighten his fellow Germans on how to interpret the Venetian style, we can hazard more than a guess about Gabrieli's intentions (bearing in mind, however, that the Germans became wildly overenthusiastic for *cori spezzati*, and were capable of elaborations of their own). Praetorius tells his readers that to find out which instruments play which music in this style, one must first look at the clef combinations of the 'choirs'. A *coro grave*, of the Gabrielian kind, merits the use of trombones or strings or possibly bassoons; a *coro superiore*, on the other hand, is just the stuff for cornetts or violins; and in case one should think that singers were totally superfluous, he is adamant that you must dispose at least one voice among each group of instruments, so that the words will not be left incomplete. As for the SATB groups marked *cappella*, all the lines must here be sung (whether they should also have instrumental support is not clear, and a matter of the interpretation of a confused chapter on the meaning of *cappella*). There are other possibilities for the use of instruments, but in the light of our knowledge of the Venetian resources and the markings on the parts of various other composers of the basilica, Praetorius gives us the elements for an interpretation which fits Giovanni's work rather well.

A motet such as 'Plaudite', for twelve voices in three choirs, begins to take on a new and more coherent form in its Praetorian colours. The clefs of the three groups give us precisely this mixture of a *coro superiore* (though its uppermost part is written in the soprano clef and does not cause any difficulty to a singer), an SATB choir, and a *coro grave*, the top part of which is written in an alto clef, the others being a tenor, baritone (F on the middle line), and bass. It could be given as a purely choral piece; but it is clear that certain voices are more vocal than others, since without singers on at least three parts, namely the lowest line of the *coro superiore*, the top part of the *coro grave*, and one tenor part

Ex. 15

of the intermediate choir, the opening bars, with their call to rejoicing, would make no sense. (See Ex. 15)

As the motet proceeds, it becomes evident that with cornetts or violins in the first, and trombones in the third choir to accompany those necessary voices, a new logic arises which makes counterpoint largely irrelevant. For the 'voice' parts are somewhat more melodious than the others, making for a duet to which the 'instruments' act as accompaniment. The concept of 'tune', of harmony derived from the melody's turn of phrase, of a texture designed to allow the voices to emerge satisfactorily, is more important. The *coro grave* is especially well written from this point of view, the alto in a penetrating part of the countertenor voice, the trombones never at theirs.

Ex. 16

We must not exaggerate the melodiousness of the supposed vocal lines: there are a number of different ways 'Plaudite' could be orchestrated to quite different effect. Nonetheless the trend towards accompanied melody is evident in such pieces, and it only requires a further step to transform this kind of music from *cori spezzati* to something quite new. This is the addition of ornaments to the 'vocal' line, to differentiate it by faster movement from the unadorned, slower gait of the instruments. That this was done in many performances of Gabrieli's early music need not be doubted, though it is only transmitted by the notation in his latest works—or rather, those works published later, for some of these need not belong to his last years. In the first Kyrie of the Mass published in 1615, for example, the alto part of a *coro grave* stands out from its fellows, probably trombones, simply by the means of *fioritura* (though they too are given embellishments from time to time).

Ex. 17

Scored in this way, how magnificent the music must have sounded; and how deeply did it impress those foreigners who had never heard the like! The English traveller Thomas Coryat heard Gabrieli's music both in St. Mark's and in the hall of the confraternity of S. Rocco, whose organist Gabrieli was for many years, in the manner of the pluralities common in Italy then as now, and from Coryat we can gain some idea of its kaleidoscopic effect, now voices, now instruments taking the attention. 'Sometimes there sung sixteene or twenty men together, having their master or moderator to keepe them in order; and when they sung, the instrumentall musitians played also. Sometimes sixeteene played together upon their instruments, ten Sagbuts, foure Cornets, and two Violdegambaes of an extraordinary greatnesse; sometimes tenne, six Sagbuts and foure Cornets; sometimes two, a Cornet and a treble violl . . .' It was indeed music that Coryat would have willingly gone 'an hundred miles a foote at any time to heare the like'. It was hearers' music; a music which would have impressed anybody, ignorant or learned in music, musical or as unmusical as Senators have a habit of being. It is a public music of the finest quality.

Yet looking at the corpus of motets contained in the first book of *Sacrae Symphoniae*, it may well be that its most fervent music is not contained in the works for three or four choirs, or those others for large forces. Certainly the most subtle pieces are built for more modest resources, and Gabrieli's professionalism, in the best sense of that word, is more readily seen in works for just two choirs, requiring the salaried singers and players of St. Mark's rather than the host of extras brought in *per diem*. Significantly it was the eight-voiced motets that the German publishers pirated so quickly after their first appearance, and which were therefore probably most often performed. It is in these that we find the greater variety of emotion and experience which can be sensed in his best organ music. The grand festival music is quite limited in what it sets out to do: it rejoices, it is splendid. But even Christmas has a tender side to its celebrations, and there is a mystery inherent in the festivals of the Blessed Virgin, however Venice might claim her for its own. It is this which Giovanni appreciates more than Andrea, more, in fact, than his colleagues Croce and Bassano and even his predecessor Merulo.

It was his Christmas motet, 'Angelus ad pastores', which seemed to continue Andrea's magnificence in the *Concerti* of 1587. Another Christmas motet from the same collection asserts Giovanni's independence. Superficially there might seem to be little difference between 'O magnum mysterium' and the grander 'Angelus ad Pastores' except one of resources. Both exploit the opposition of high and low tessitura, both have extended allelujas, both have the succinctness of the best writing for *cori spezzati*. It is only when the two are heard in close proximity that 'O magnum mysterium' reveals what has been lacking in the larger work: for at once the subtlety of its harmony creates a richness of feeling far beyond that of Gabrieli's grander conceptions. The fact is that the larger the resources, the more simple the harmony usually is. Tonic-dominant progressions dominate extensive tracts of the music for a dozen or more voices. Reduce the number of parts to eight and immediately the obvious can be avoided. 'O magnum mysterium' has a magical opening section simply because it is based on the opposition of major and minor. Certainty has vanished, the mystery of the Virgin birth is emphasized by the continual doubt as to the nature of the next chord. Even when the cadence at the end of the paragraph for one choir seems to have achieved satisfaction in the major, the second choir quickly disperses it with a recurrence—quite logical since the piece begins so—of the opening minor chord. And as the work progresses, it is noticeable that the second choir gives an unexpected twist to the phrase so as to leave it on a dominant chord, in preparation for a tutti in which the harmonies are gorgeously enriched by thick inner counterpoints. There is comparatively little of Andrea's brilliance in this piece, for even the alleluja has that dancing quality we have seen in 'Hodie Christus

Ex. 18

natus est' rather than the stolid rhythms of earlier music. There are other motets where it is still less in evidence, Giovanni is especially fine at creating almost sombre moods by harmonic means. 'O Domine Jesu Christe', to take an example which is justly one of his most popular works today, does not seem remarkable from a technical point of view, though Gabrieli uses suspensions quite freely. But again, the way it is never certain that the discord will resolve on a major or minor tonality, or whether indeed the phrase will be extended by still further dissonance, creates a highly emotional atmosphere, most appropriate to the contemplation of Christ crucified.

Ex. 19

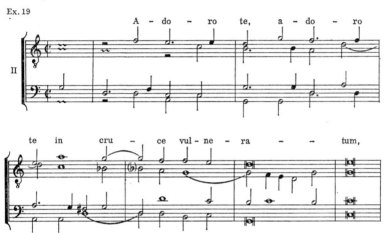

If it is harmony which is the key to Giovanni's expressions of passion, it is his mastery of rhythm and phrase that allow him to convey that shading of feeling we have noticed in his organ music. The problem of rhythm was acute for many sixteenth-century composers. With a trend towards syllabic setting of words, strongly backed not only by the theorists in the humanist tradition but by the clerics of the Council of Trent, that suppleness which the contrapuntists had readily available often disappeared. The short masses of such men as Ruffo and Croce are at times surprisingly jog-trot, in the same way that the services of the earlier Anglicans can be. Setting Italian, Giovanni was not as resourceful as were many of his contemporaries; in Latin he seems more at home, and it is rare for him not to find a natural way of accentuation. He is aided by two discoveries. The first is that since in madrigals one can put a syllable on as short a note as a crochet, there is no reason why it cannot be done quite freely in church music, something about which older composers were comparatively cautious (though Andrea was one of the more daring). The second discovery was that syncopation could not only be used for musical excitement but also to give a more exact declamation. Doubtless Giovanni's predilection for off-beat accents came from Lasso in the first place; it was certainly increased by the nature of *cori spezzati*, whereby one choir picks up from the other immediately after the accented tonic chord of the cadence, giving an anacrusis.

Ex. 20
Jubilate Deo (1597)

Integrate this into melody, rather than just using it as part of the interchange of choirs, and a new plasticity arises, unknown to composers who are bound by the doctrine of an accented first note of the phrase.

Ex. 21
Domine Dominus Noster (1597)

These things give a fluency to the music which is extremely useful in dealing with some of the longer texts, while musically remaining comparatively brief, as festal circumstances demand. They also lead to a freedom of dialogue that can be the true virtue of the double choir. Andrea was skilled in manipulating his forces so that there was a delicious uncertainty about the source of the next phrase. Sometimes he worked in long sentences, especially at the beginning of a motet, as though he, like Willaert, felt that he had to preserve the verbal unit; then he suddenly alternated his choirs in short, pithy phrases, often no more than two or three chords, to create a sense of climax, even though the text might suggest more extended writing. It is an art in which Giovanni excelled from the start. 'O magnum mysterium' is a cardinal example of unpredictability, for after the remarkably regular phrases of its opening section, choir can interrupt choir, impeding a steady flow, or can extend an idea in a rapturous contemplation. In some motets this becomes even more subtle. The eight-voiced 'Beati omnes' opens with a paragraph of eight bars for one choir; its fellow replies with a shorter section of three bars and then they join together for three more bars. This is quite in Andrea's manner. But it is now that the real dialogue is joined. The first choir sings 'quam manducabis' to receive the usual reply 'beatus es'—which is then taken up by the first choir; this idea is not abandoned, for Choir II perseveres with it, and there is a continual development both of this brief phrase and its reply 'et bene tibi erit', in both choirs separately and then together.

Ex. 22

Nearly every musical idea throughout the motet is treated in this way, now being broken off, now being extended into a flowing section; and the simple idea of one choir succeeding the other in an orderly fashion has been totally left behind. It is the art of conversation, as opposed to the successive set speeches of stiffer works for *cori spezzati*.

It is this malleability in harmony, melody, and dialogue which makes Giovanni Gabrieli's double choir music so expressive, so full of the variety lacking in previous exponents of this medium. At its best, it is capable of marvels. In yet one more Christmas motet, the word genius can hardly be denied him. 'O Jesu mi dulcissime' again evokes the scene in the manger, and its opening fourteen bars for a *coro grave* shows a mastery of rich harmony. 'Adoro te', on the other hand, tautens the rhythms and soon there is genuine dialogue. Repetitions are rarely exact, and at a climax for 'O divina ergo', what seems to be a simple inflation of a chordal block suddenly reveals a new tonal direction pointed by an apparently innocent flourish by the tenor of Choir II. And the rapture of the piece comes to its light in an astonishing chromatic change: not academic, as chromaticism often was in the 1560s and 1570s, not chaotically Gesualdian, but a masterstroke precisely because it comes out of the blue.

Ex. 23

This is not the work of a splendour-loving Venetian, rejoicing in the Republic's glory. If a label can be put on it, it is a Counter-Reformation piece, subtle and rich, marvellous and emotional. When it was first published Gabrieli was in his early forties, and a master; but there is more mastery to come, and 'O Jesu mi dulcissime' shows where the way forward was to lead.

THE INSTRUMENTAL MUSIC

IF Giovanni could build on the work of his predecessors in composing festal church music, no one could teach him how to write festal instrumental music; for no one had composed much of it. There were the canzonas and ricercars of his uncle, of course, but these were almost all for a small ensemble of no more than four instruments. It was, in fact, only after Giovanni's return to Venice in the 1580s that the grand ensemble of St. Mark's began to be built up. It was as late as 1567 that the basilica had its own permanent group of players at all, and then it was only some three wind players from Udine. In 1576, a brilliant young cornettist, Giovanni Bassano, was added, and in the early 1580s after the change of duke in Munich, one or two virtuosi who visited Venice were snapped up by the Procurators, until there were six salaried instrumentalists. In addition to these, the treasurer of St. Mark's was, from 1581, empowered to hire additional players *per diem* as required. This power he seems to have delegated to the *maestro di cappella*, who, in Giovanni's earliest years, seems to have delegated it in turn to the young organist. Giovanni liked having a dozen or fifteen of these extras for an important festival, and there were often more than twenty players in St Mark's. That their principal duties were in swelling the sound of the motets may be taken for granted; but having them in church was too good an opportunity to be missed, and Giovanni began to write pieces for them without the voices, to be performed perhaps as an *entrata* or at the elevation of the host or as a *post communio*. That this was largely Giovanni's doing may be gauged from the fact that whereas he wrote some three dozen pieces for this ensemble, nobody else seems to have done so: not Donato or Croce, *maestri di cappella*, or even Bassano, director of the instrumentalists in his mature years, of whose festal instrumental music we possess literally none. So, not unlike Haydn, whose isolation at Eisenstadt forced him to solve his problems without recourse to others' experience, Gabrieli, by force of circumstances, became original.

Not that it might seem so at first sight. The works which apparently are novel, being called 'sonata' (a term used but a few times in the period before 1597), on examination turn out to be Willaertian ricercars in a new guise. Probably Gabrieli did not call them that in view of the scholarly connotation which that word was acquiring. The rest are canzonas, the commonest of all instrumental genres. But what canzonas these are! There is nothing of their quality in the repertoire of Italian ensemble music either during their time, or indeed more than half a century to come. The obvious method of approach for Gabrieli in the composition of large scale works was to follow the pattern of the *cori spezzati* motet. So of the sixteen instrumental pieces included in the *Sacrae Symphoniae* of 1597, ten are for double 'choir' and three more are for three groups, after the manner of 'Plaudite' or the grand mass settings. The musical resources of the motet are also deployed in these pieces. There is the same mastery of phrase, the same command of harmony, the same malleability of texture; which in turn means that there is the same emotional breadth and variety. Those for whom a canzona meant a gay French chanson, or even one of Andrea's *ricercari ariosi*, must have found the bleak music of the 'Canzon Noni Toni' (no. 4 of the *Sacrae Symphoniae*) very strange. It is a study in the minor. The opening section of some eight bars for the first 'choir' contains scarcely three major chords—and these are dominant on their way to tonic chords. It is no better when the other 'choir' joins in. There is an 'alleluja' in triple time; and this is a bleak affair too.

Ex. 24

When this is finished, there is what seems to be a quotation of the bittersweet harmonies of 'Lieto godea' (see Example 7 *supra*). The show of energy as this is continued proves to be illusory, as the alleluja comes back. Indeed, after yet another rather cheerless episode, it is this re-frain which brings the piece to an end. We may well ask what festival this was designed for. It sounds more like penitential music for Holy Week than something for Venice's gorgeous processionals.

At the other extreme, could anything be more festive than the 'Can-zon Septimi Toni' (no. 3 of the *Sacrae Symphoniae*), which fizzes with a champagne quality from the opening note? The chanson motif is given a simple diatonic harmony, the dialogue is joined immediately as one choir takes up the phrase of the other. In the fourth bar, there are some splendid military rhythms which remind us that Andrea's scanty large-scale instrumental music included a *battaglia*, or battle piece, made from fanfares and other such elementary devices.

The triple-time section on this occasion is a genuinely happy affair, full of major chords and perfect cadences, and the duples which separate its

Ex. 25

statement from another near the end have rhythms which tumble over each other with joy. Sequences abound, choir continues to repeat choir, the climaxes are sonorous, the dialogue vigorous and well argued.

The means are those of the motet, but the moods and attitudes of both these pieces emphasize that Gabrieli's instrumental music is concerned with things inexpressible in vocal terms. The blackness of the 'Canzon Noni Toni' comes about because it does not need the contrasts which words were bound to suggest to some degree, and thus concentrates on a particular aspect of its mode. The 'Canzon Septimi Toni' similarly achieves its happiness by rhythms which, in the normal way, words would be bound to frustrate. Indeed, its whole melodic shaping is truly instrumental, a term which now needs definition. The stuff of instrumental music in the sixteenth century was the dance. There can be little doubt that most instrumentalists spent much of their energy in playing dances (when a Doge was elected there was often a week of celebrations including lengthy *balli*). Dances are by their nature strongly and regularly accented; they need also to be homophonic in texture. Thus instrumental technique places emphasis on clear articulation rather than on the subtleties of melody. Then looking at Bassano's tutor on ornamentation, it seems likely that the cornettist, at least, learned to play his instruments by practising scales and other sequential patterns. This is a natural way of educating the fingers and will give them preferences for certain melodic tags which again are not necessarily those of the contrapuntist. It is this clarity of rhythm and tendency towards the sequence which informs much of Gabrieli's ensemble music and makes it deliciously hummable.

The 'Canzon Primi Toni', the first of the instrumental pieces of the *Sacrae Symphoniae*, is for these reasons quite irresistible. Its first four-bar phrase, with its sequences and strong articulation of the chanson motto which turns into a dance, is hard to dismiss from the memory. So good is the tune that Gabrieli repeats it note for note on the second 'choir'—and then, like a chanson composer, repeats the whole section, so that we have heard the tune four times. The dialogue intensifies, and there is some virtuosity in the cornett parts (for so they must be), simply because the only method of making a climax after this swinging melody is to break into semiquavers; and there are the customary triples. Then comes a curious ending, for though the cornetts continue displaying their dexterity, their *fioritura* does not seem quite to fit the chords of their colleagues, leaving a sense of indecision rather at odds with the brightness of the canzona's opening.

The florid nature of these upper parts emphasizes the nature of St.

Ex. 26

Mark's ensemble with its salaried virtuosi and its *per diem* ripieni. Another work shows even more surely that Gabrieli has pondered the best deployment of such forces. It is a canzona for ten 'voices', given in alternative versions. The first of these demands four cornetts and a trombone in each of its two choirs, and seems to be an essay in the grand motet manner, for not only does it open with a sonorous tutti, there is also a distinct lack of the usual tunefulness. There is more counterpoint in it, more ornaments passed between the cornetts, and generally greater elaboration and thickness of texture. It is only on turning to the second version that all becomes plain. This version is marked 'Canzon in Echo Duodecimi Toni' and opens with a tutti as does the other. But after nine bars the tutti disappears and we are left with just two cornetts, the cantus parts of the two 'choirs'. These are each to be accompanied by an organ (the part was never printed by Gardano but the intention is clear) and one cornett echoes the other—more or less, since occasionally the 'echo' initiates the material and since Giovanni Gabrieli never allows a sterile device to get in the way of the music. Soon the tutti is brought back, and though it does not repeat its opening section, the fact that it uses the canzona rhythms gives an immediate feeling of unity. There are five solo sections in all, with intermediate and concluding tuttis. It is, in fact, a concerto movement, primitive by the standards of Vivaldi since there is no concept of varied tonality, but a concerto nonetheless. It is not the most interesting of Gabrieli's instrumental works, but it does show the way his mind was working; and it shows also that the beginnings of the concerto lie in late sixteenth-century Venice.

This work demonstrates, as does the best of the organ music, Gabrieli's intuitive understanding that the essence of instrumental music lies in formal patterns to replace the unifying nature of words. It is this sense which Gabrieli developed in his later instrumental music to an astonishing degree. The next of his instrumental pieces to be published were included in an anthology compiled by an ambitious publisher, Raverio, in 1608, and though some are quite early works, there are a couple of canzonas which stylistically belong to the first years of the century. Of these, a canzona subtitled 'Fa, sol, la, re' is an extraordinary piece. Canzona? It is in triple time almost throughout, and seems to have lost the usual motto rhythm completely; and the subtitle refers to the solmization syllables (the tonic sol-fa of its day) of its principal theme—which is in the bass. It looks indeed like one of these new-fangled ostinato pieces which the moderns were so fond of, and the pattern is indeed very close to that of Monteverdi's famous duet 'Chiome d'oro' of the next decade.

Ex. 27

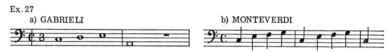
a) GABRIELI   b) MONTEVERDI

But this is no scholarly investigation of the potentialities of a ground bass. The excitement comes in the very unpredictability of its repetitions. At the opening it comes only in the third bar; there are three whole bars before it arrives to clinch the next cadence; but then a gap of a single bar suffices before its next entry. Later it is deployed continually, without any break, to make it a genuine ostinato. Then it is allowed something of a rest, as the tune above it develops. Moreover, it changes its nature. Its original entry is in A *minor*: transpose it down a third and it strongly supports F *major*. C major is not out of bounds, nor is D minor, and because of its shape, wherever it goes there is a feeling of a perfect cadence. So the canzona sweeps from one tonality to another, sometimes lingering in one, sometimes dashing through on its way elsewhere. It is as closely argued as a sonata movement by Haydn. Yet the innocent ear would remember only the tune in the upper parts and the splendour of sound—sound as festive as ever, made from the bright colours of the upper instruments which dominate the scene.

The title of 'canzona' in the posthumously published *Canzoni et Sonate* (1615) often merits an interrogation mark, for these pieces leave far behind the simplicities of even the relatively sophisticated works of 1597. There are other works in triples, dance- rather than song-like, and when the motto opening is maintained it is more often a gesture than a reality. Gabrieli often sticks to the outward appearance of *cori spezzati*, taking its suggestions of contrasting colours in various ways. That he had two superb cornettists is evident from many pieces (Bassano was still with the basilica at Gabrieli's death); and now he had two, sometimes three greatly talented violinists, whom Coryat heard and thought very marvellous (being English he describes them as treble viols, but that they were violinists is proved by the account books). So Gabrieli quite often has the upper parts of his double choirs in contrasting sonorities. But *cori spezzati* technique is not now his primary interest. This has become vested in melody and, as we might expect, intricate formal patterning. Whether it was the excellence of his cornettists and violinists, or the influence of the new music with basso continuo, which even conservative Venice could not ignore for long, Gabrieli becomes in these last works a supreme melodist. In 'Canzon XI', to take one of the most agreeable works in the 1615 collection, there is some suggestion of counterpoint at the opening, but the cornetts of the first choir soon take over to build a paragraph of a dozen bars before there is any hint of *spezzato* dialogue. The interchanges are then brief, and the violins of Choir II sweetly develop their own sequential tune; and so it proceeds in the large units necessary to create such melodiousness, the interchanges acting as a rondo refrain. At times cornett will echo cornett or a violin, violin; but these effects are within the single group, not hailed from one gallery of St. Mark's to another. Throughout most of the canzonas, in fact, the true dialogue lies in the duets between like instruments, a usage developed from the 'modern' madrigal, rapidly becoming popular in most genres, not least the chamber duet.

At the very end of Canzon XI, Gabrieli breaks into his former brilliance, with the ornamental cadence, in which the cornetts and violins display their *fioritura* over some simple, slow-moving chords. Not only is this *fioritura* very different from that of his earlier pieces, but in other ways there has been a distinct change of attitude. For one thing, the very ornamental figures are more complex than of old. Complicated dotted rhythms and several really fast-moving embellishments are now commonplace, and several of the violin parts are especially brilliant. There is some appreciation of the thinking of those theorists of monodic song, that continuous passage work is less effective than the short, crisp ornament to crown a phrase, though it is remarkable how Gabrieli integrates ornaments into his melodic strands. A sort of turn in Canzon XV, by being repeated five times, seems less an attempt at display by the violins than a natural sequential climax to a duet.

Ex. 28

Vln. $\frac{1}{2}$

[The lower parts are omitted]

If it is such things which make these canzonas so obviously attractive to any listener, it is their mastery of form which must inspire the
admiration of the professional musician. There are fairly simple rondo
patterns in Canzon XI and Sonata XIII (which has clearly been mis-
named by Gabrieli's editor), the latter strongly related to the 'alleluja'
rondo motet, which gives it a particularly gracious attractiveness. Yet
these works seem totally unsophisticated compared with Canzon XVII,
written for three choirs, in each of which the upper instruments are a
cornett and a violin (presumably the lower ones are trombones). It
opens with a fanfare.

Ex. 29

Violin

Cornett

Could anything be more innocent? Yet virtually the whole eighty-five
bars of the work comes in one way or another from the first four notes.
The second choir adds new harmonizations, the first choir replying
with inversions in the bass. Later, there are diminutions, and versions
with exciting syncopations, and while the final flourishes are provided
by the upper instruments, the eye at least perceives yet one more
variant, developed in canon by the lower instruments of the three
groups. In the few moments when there are no such links, there are
hints of a rondo pattern embodied in a cadential formula. It is an
astonishing work.

So is Canzon VIII; and whereas there is a hint of primitive joy in the fanfares of Canzon XVII, here we are back to the darker hues of the impassioned Gabrieli. It is scored for *coro superiore*—three cornetts and a trombone perhaps—and a *coro grave*, surely of trombones, and it seems at the opening to be the nearest we can find to the older *cori spezzati* canzona, leading off brilliantly with the motto in counterpoint on the upper instruments. In the fifth bar there is an apparent link to allow the deep choir to enter.

Ex. 30

At this stage it is not very noteworthy, and only when the second group ends its section with it at a lower octave does it acquire any significance. Thereafter, it is ubiquitous. It is played by either group singly or by both together; it is sometimes grand, sometimes reticent. Being constructed with a terminal dominant chord, it can lead to any kind of new material without interrupting the flow. There are sombre triple-time passages, intense dialogue in the old way, brilliant paragraphs full of ornaments, dynamic counterpoint. And at the conclusion, Gabrieli has to state it twice, on the full ensemble, for no one would otherwise believe the piece at an end.

The fact that the cornetts which in these works are needful have only recently been revived, and that the ensemble is totally unlike the modern orchestra, have ensured more than three and a half centuries of neglect for these splendid pieces, which shows that posterity is no refined judge, but sometimes just a butcher. For there is no doubt that there is enormous emotional variety and intellectual quality in this music, in some ways outdoing the grander church music on which has rested Gabrieli's fame in modern times. There is irony also in the fact that the only instrumental work of his to be truly well known has achieved its reputation for the wrong reasons. The 'Sonata pian e forte' is supposedly the earliest work to use expression marks; and this is hardly proven, since Banchieri had published music using the same terms in 1596, a year before Gabrieli's appeared. Then, with the other 'sonatas', this is said to be the beginning of the sonata tradition; but nomenclature is no sure guide in the sixteenth century, and Gabrieli's sonatas are in style the most backward-looking of his ensemble music. Not that they are the worse for that; they are indeed splendid, and some of the finest works he ever wrote. This very 'Sonata pian e forte', though not the best of them, is excellent music. The scoring, two choirs each of three trombones and a 'melody' instrument, seeks contrast only in the difference between *violino* (in this context a viola) and cornett. It is a study in dark hues, and the big 'white' notes of the motet dominate the first section to add to the solemnity. As for the famous expression marks, they seem to be a guide to the player to tell him only that he must be soft in single choir, loud in tutti, and the long phrases for each choir in turn cause an even more subdued atmosphere. Suddenly, the dialogue is joined, the quietness interrupted by a grand forte, and from then on, we feel that the dimly lit embers can at any time burst into a bright flame. Now the markings are not confined to emphasizing single choir versus tutti, but act as contrasting elements in their own right. There is a magnificent moment when the first choir broods over a suspension in long quiet notes while the second pounces with dynamic, forte, black notes, before it too resumes the brooding.

Perhaps the only disappointment in the piece is its conclusion, some

Ex. 31

Lasso-type contrapuntal working out of a cliché of no great distinction. But the greatest of the sonatas are surely those written for huge resources. In the 1597 *Sacrae Symphoniae* the last of the instrumental pieces is a 'Canzon Quinti Toni' for fifteen 'voices'; on examination this turns out to be no gay or even sad canzona, but clearly a sonata—an instrumental motet if ever there was one. The scoring again is rich. There are three choirs of five strands, four of which in each choir are marked for trombones. The upper three parts are for two cornetts and a *violino*. The emphasis is once more on sombreness, on the minor chord, the long, inexorable phrase, the gradually rising excitement as the three-way dialogue becomes animated. It is a masterwork in the *cori spezzati* manner, with textures more polyphonic than usual, and the resulting harmony more profound. Crimson rather than scarlet, it shows Gabrieli at his most intense and satisfying.

Of the five so-called 'sonatas' of the 1615 collection, one is really a canzona and another is a concertante work the discussion of which does not belong here. The three remaining works follow the lines of the sonatas of the earlier era. They are in certain respects distinctly backward looking. Their principal interest still lies in *spezzato* dialogue rather than the complex formal pattern of the canzona, though the integration and development of themes comes so naturally to Gabrieli by this time that unifying devices are not hard to detect. They are also rather more contrapuntal than most canzonas, and certainly they have a gravity about them. They are big works, in feeling, in resource, in length. They do not neglect the new entirely, and their use of ornaments is every bit as interesting as that of the canzonas. If on paper this seems to give them more brilliance than the earlier sonatas, this is somewhat illusory in performance. The Sonata XIX uses the same fifteen strands as the 1597 'canzona', and though there are no precise indications for instruments, the clefs denote the same twelve trombones, with cornetts and perhaps a *violino*. There is the same steady tread, as long sections for single choir gradually grow into an animated dialogue. There is the same intensity of harmony, more dissonant than would be usual in a canzona, and the phrase lengths are unpredictable, as Gabrieli displays the contrapuntist's skill at avoiding cadences. It is first the hint of a unifying theme which projects the argument from one choir to another that reminds us that this is Gabrieli's high maturity; and then the ornaments of the upper instruments passed from one to another, becoming more and more virtuosic, tell of the result of his by now long experience. Its nobility is the quintessence of Venice; its fierceness of emotion the quintessence of Gabrieli.

THE FINAL PHASE

WITH the death of Doge Grimani at Christmas time in 1605, Venice entered troubled waters. A quarrel with Papal Rome, already serious, nearly resulted in war a year later, and then actually caused the excommunication of the Republic and its citizens until its resolution in 1607. When this quarrel subsided, though Venice seemed to have won, there was an unease for which the contemporary chroniclers could find only minor causes; but nonetheless, the days of glory were over. Reading between the lines of Procuratorial minutes, the *cappella* at St. Mark's was in some neglect also. Gabrieli told a Mantuan sent to find musicians for the Gonzaga household that there was not a really good alto in Venice, and it is noticeable that for the grand annual festivals at the Scuola Grande di S. Rocco he used to import singers from Padua. The principal composers of the *cappella* were ageing: Croce, Bassano, and Gabrieli were fifty or over, and Gabrieli himself was suffering from a kidney stone which kept him away from the basilica from time to time. It may be that he also felt somewhat out of touch with musical events, for it was around this period that Venice became fully aware of the revolution which had been taking place for the last twenty years. Most probably it was the discussions over Monteverdi's notorious *Fifth Book of Madirgals* which caused this knowledge rather than the products of the monodic style, the New Music of Caccini and Peri, for these remained in distant Florence, whereas Monteverdi's music caused a public row and wide publicity.

A fifty-year-old conservative might be expected to ignore such things. On the contrary, there are signs that Gabrieli was interested, not in everything the new school of composition was attempting, but in various ideas and technical devices that it was investigating. One sign lies in the music of his pupils. He was now a famous teacher, and many dukes and princes in Northern Europe sent young men to study organ and composition with him. Before they left, each seems to have composed a book of Italian madrigals under his direction; and what madrigals these are! The model is not the sedate manner of Gabrieli's own secular music, but the work of the moderns. These are violent pieces, often dissonant, sometimes chromatic. They set the latest vogue in verse, passionate, even indecently sexual poems of the sort which

Gabrieli had never touched. Yet the music of these foreigners—Pedersøn, Nielson, Grabbe, Schütz—is never quite Italian avant-garde. It is too selfconsciously contrapuntal, and lacks the conciseness of the Monteverdian composers, their wit and dramatic sense. Even so, it shows a surprisingly thorough knowledge of the musical symbolism and technical resource of the latest madrigals.

Gabrieli's own music shows the same, and more. Admittedly, not all of his music by any means. There are conventional enough works, such as the huge 'Audite principes' for sixteen voices, in the posthumous collections, which may yet belong to his final years. There are less conventional works which have nothing to do with the moderns, but are essentially developed from his older style. One magnificent motet, 'Suscipe', written for the feast of St. John the Baptist, at first sight looks novel simply because only six of its twelve parts have words provided, the others being marked 'trombone'. It is not really so new: it has, in fact, two *cori gravi*, one of men's voices, the other of instruments, and this is not very far from earlier works, though the fact that there is no voice of any kind in the second choir breaks away from Praetorius's rules. The novelty lies in the treatment of these resources, which is extraordinarily skilled, for instead of pitting one choir against the other, Gabrieli writes a series of duets for the voices—first two altos, then the tenors, finally the basses, accompanying them with the trombones. It would be easy to drown the voices, since their highest notes are too low

Ex. 32

immensae majes - ta - - - tis

to penetrate a thick texture. This Gabrieli avoids by keeping the trombones in the least brilliant part of their compass; and when, at the climax, he needs all the voices and all the trombones, his technique is to play solemn slow-moving chords on the trombones, while the singers are allowed more florid lines.

There are other methods, such as those in the magnificent 'O Jesu Christe' and 'Domine, Dominus meus', again written modestly for a dark-hued men's choir; these vary the older manner by the addition of ornaments which make the mood even more serious by their brief, but significant dissonance. There are others where the instruments to be used are marked, such as the splendid 'Jubilate Deo'. They are in actual sound not very different from early pieces, though the refrain of the rondo in this motet is separated by passages for small, variable groups of singers rather than the block choirs of *cori spezzati*.

Nonetheless, the new means inspire him, and are responsible for some fine music. He found the *basso continuo* especially useful. Like Monteverdi, he saw in it a device less for allowing the solo singer more rhythmic licence, or for cutting down the numbers of performers, which had been the aim of its inventors, than for giving a further contrast—that between the accompanied voice and a grand tutti. The superb Christmas motet 'Quem vidistis pastores' owes much of its variety to this discovery. The layout of his forces is ostensibly that for double choir, each group consisting of four instruments and three voices, but from the start the conventions are ignored. It is the instruments of both choirs which play the opening sinfonia, and whether they are *spezzati* or not is almost irrelevant. Then comes the first solo section in which the bass of Choir I, accompanied by the organ, sings some eight bars in which the proposition of the words is put. The soprano of the same choir, also accompanied by the organ, extends the idea over a dozen bars, whereupon the tenor of Choir II takes over the burden—and so on, until each singer has had a turn. This fills some eighty-five bars, and though most of the melody has been straightforward enough (it might almost be a strand in a contrapuntal motet), first ornaments, then chromaticisms heighten the tension. Now Gabrieli writes a duet for tenors; and here the Monteverdian influence is strong, since in style it is extraordinarily near to the last six madrigals of that composer's Fifth Book, where the *basso continuo* is essential, and the wreathing, encrusted melody is brought forth. (Ex. 33.)

So it continues with the soloists and the keyboard until the words 'O magnum mysterium' take Gabrieli back to well-trodden paths: and one cannot help but admire and be moved by the old sonorities. They are

Ex. 33

made grander by the occasional ornaments and a powerful sequential lift of a tone at the climax, but in essence still show Andrea's doxological magnificence. Though the rapture of the ornamented quasi-contrapuntal strands belongs to Giovanni's maturity, and his octave doubling in the 'alleluja', in place of elaborate polyphony, is that of the seventeenth-century composer rather than Andrea.

That Gabrieli should find a technical device useful is not particularly surprising. It is much more unexpected to discover his acceptance of the basic idea underlying the New Music: *prima le parole, poi la musica*. 'Acceptance' is probably too strong a word, 'cognizance' more appropriate, for Gabrieli certainly does not adopt the negative attitude (musically speaking) implied by the Florentines. Still, it is strange that so 'pure' a musician, so restrained a madrigalist, should begin to use the extravagances of the moderns. His harmonic language has become noticeably free. Passing dissonances frequently do not progress by step, and explanations of this must be of the same kind that Monteverdi gave for his own transgressions of the academic rules; in effect, that either the discords are ornamental or that they express the inner meaning of the words. The first explanation will do for the moment in the setting of 'Jubilate Deo' already mentioned, where a chord of G seems to have been superimposed on one of F, for all is satisfactorily resolved on the next chord, and with a little sophistry the passing notes can be said to find niches somewhere in it. The second explanation is needed for a small but highly significant number of works in which the new philosophy calls all in doubt.

The best known of these today is a motet published in the *Reliquae Sacrorum*, 'Timor et tremor'. The text might indeed be from a *madrigale spirituale*, full of emotional words, and at the opening, strong images.

Timor et tremor venerunt super me,	Fear and trembling have come over me,
et caligo cecidit super me:	and darkness fell upon me:
miserere mei, Domine,	take pity upon me, Lord,
quoniam in te confidit anima mea.	because my soul trusts in Thee.
Exaudi, Deus, deprecationem meam,	God, grant my prayer,
quia refugium meum es tu et	for Thou art my refuge and
adjutor fortis.	strong helper.
Domine, invocavi te,	Lord, I have called upon Thee,
non confundar in aeternum.	Let me not for ever be confounded.

Gabrieli's setting is astonishing by any standards. 'Timor' is expressed by two favourite devices of the modern school: a downward sixth in the most prominent melodic strands, as in the 'Lamento d'Arianna', and a break between the two syllables of the word in the way common in expressing a lover's sigh—so-spi-ro—in a pastoral madrigal. The 'tremor' provides an ornamental figure which will not be found recommended as normal practice in the treatises of Bassano, da Udine, or even by Caccini. Put these together and the effect is extraordinary; how extraordinary may be savoured in Manfred Bukofzer's comparison[1] with a setting of these same words by Andrea not many decades earlier. There are more marvels to come, including a chromatic triple-time section to express the closing phrase of the text, a kind of avant-gardist's 'alleluja', the rhythms suggesting joy which the melody and resultant harmonies promptly deny. But perhaps the most remarkable

[1] *Music in the Baroque Era* (London, 1948).

Exaudi Deus (1565) Andrea Gabrieli

Ex. 34(b)

Giovanni Gabrieli

feature of the motet is its huge scale. It is not, in truth, a spiritual madrigal, for domestic use only, but a grand choral piece, a public statement of emotion. Its development of material is, like that in the German pupils' madrigals, the work of a great contrapuntist with a sense of sonority rather than the concise, living-for-the-moment madrigalist.

This point is made even more clearly in another 'advanced' piece, the setting of the psalm 'Exaudi me'. 'Advanced' hardly seems the right word on regarding its four choirs, two of high, two of low tessitura, though a lack of treble clefs may suggest that this is not to be one of Giovanni's more brilliant pieces.

The first choir sets off in conventional enough counterpoint, and only an occasional ornamental figure disturbs the calm. Then comes the word 'tremenda', and the ornament, if it may so be described in this context, makes its point. The next interruption of the flow is the 'sigh' for the word 'movendi', a 'double sigh' in fact, since there are three syllables to the word. By this time, all is in the melting pot and

the word 'tremens' takes us completely into the mood of 'Timor et tremor'. When four choirs echo around the church with broken melody for the phrase 'quando caeli movendi sunt', an emotional cataclysm has happened.

'Exaudi me' is a huge work in every sense; but if it therefore belongs firmly to traditional Venetian ways, its use of madrigalian symbolism has wrought a great change. Perhaps the only analogous transformation at this time can be found in the superb conclusion to the prayer to the Blessed Virgin, 'Audi caelum', and the Magnificat settings, in Monteverdi's Vespers music of 1610. Though some minor Venetians try something similar, notably one Giovanni Francesco Cappello, whose *Lamentations* of these same years essay a 'secular' manner, there is nothing with this grandeur of emotional scale.

It would be ironic to make out Giovanni Gabrieli as a revolutionary in the end—and quite wrong. Such works are few, and there are more where the new techniques are put to traditional Venetian purposes. It is appropriate to conclude a survey of Gabrieli's church music with one of these. 'In ecclesiis' has been one of the most reprinted of his motets, and deservedly so, for it is a splendid piece. There are obvious traditional features; a text of rejoicing, the rondo shape made by an alleluja refrain, forces grouped into three choirs. There are obvious innovations. The three choirs are not quite of the same disposition as of old. One is admittedly marked *cappella* and has the usual SATB constitution; but there is another group of voices who sing for the most part to an organ accompaniment; and the third choir is the instrumental ensemble, three cornetts, a *violino* (in practice a viola), and two trombones. Then the actual treatment of the 'choirs' hardly belongs to the old *cori spezzati* dialogue. Instead, the solo singers (as surely the first group of voices must be, given the weakness of the St. Mark's choir at the time) set off with miniature arias and duets, not fully shaped and developed, it is true, but nevertheless sections more or less complete in themselves. These singers are allowed *fioritura*, while the *cappella* is confined to simple allelujas in block chords. The instruments play a short sinfonia, beginning with the canzona motto, then proceeding with bouncing, quasi-military dotted rhythms; and with a flash of genius, Giovanni does not begin his motet with this, but makes it but anticipate the final chord of an alleluja to take us by surprise. The grand climax shows still more genius. Arriving at the prayer 'Deus, Deus meus, adjutor noster' Giovanni remembers yet again his uncle's settings of the doxology, with their grand, solemn chords. His chords are every bit as sonorous, exploiting the whole range of voice and instrument, but harmonically

Ex. 36

Andrea's simple dominants and tonics are left far behind. First one
chromatic change, then another, transforms the whole atmosphere, and
finally the grandeur carries on in a passage of unique splendour. While
the instruments and the *cappella* sustain a dominant pedal, the soloists
flaunt the quasi-improvised flourishes for bar after bar, as though the
motet's full glory will never end.

'Motet' seems the wrong word for 'In ecclesiis'. In so many ways
does it remind us of the future that 'cantata' appears more appropriate.
There are the solos, the distinct sectionalism of the orchestral symphony,
the choral interjections all of which will be developed throughout the
seventeenth century. No longer does the spatial element matter very
much. 'In ecclesiis' would go as happily in the Scuola di S. Rocco
where Gabrieli also played the organ, with its oblong hall, as in St.
Mark's, for the contrasts are now inherent in the media. The particular circumstances have at last given way to the general. Thus Gabrieli has
moved away from a backwater of musical history, into the main stream.

THE VERDICT OF POSTERITY

He died in mid-August 1612 and in his native city was promptly for-
gotten. When Monteverdi died thirty years later, Venice, we are told,

went into mourning: there is no sign of any similar gesture for Gabrieli. His successor in St. Mark's was a nonentity, and at the confraternity of S. Rocco one of his own pupils was little better. Monteverdi came to Venice a year later, and thereafter Venetian music followed new paths. Yet we sense that Giovanni had been a remarkable human being, for his friends gathered up his music, and in 1615 the great posthumous collections appeared. His pupils loved him. Schütz, the last of them, had been given a ring by his master while Giovanni was on his deathbed and though he was to live another sixty years he never forgot his pupillage. 'Ye Gods, what a man he was', he wrote years later of Giovanni. But it was Schütz's music which was to be his greatest tribute. His *Psalms of David* were published in 1619, and though the German language gives a squareness to his rhythms as opposed to those of Giovanni's more supple melodic lines, the alleluja refrains are unmistakably Gabrielian. Nor did he forget that other great lesson of Giovanni's final years—that of intense setting of intense words. Listening to his setting—published in 1623 with that of others—of Psalm 116 contained in a collection called *Angst der Hellen und Friede der Seelen* (which might be translated as *The Pains of Hell and the Contentment of the Soul*), we find that same mood, the same attitude, as in 'Timor et tremor'. And herein lies the paradox. Throughout the seventeenth century, Italian music was becoming less dependent on the words, was developing new formal patterns in instrumental music, both features of Giovanni's earlier church music and of the great canzonas. Yet here his influence and fame were naught. The Germans knew his later music and followed paths which were not entirely characteristic of his total *oeuvre*. His influence here was immense. It is no accident that North of the Alps the grand polychoral manner still flourished at a time when it had almost completely disappeared in Italy; nor that it was in Germany that the 'theory of the affections', that is, the way to match emotions inherent in poetic texts by musical figures of various kinds, was to be taken so seriously. It is no accident that J. S. Bach, a hundred years after Gabrieli's death, was still writing double-choir motets, and was much concerned with an intricate language of musical images, which, if somewhat exaggerated by Schweitzer, was an essential part of his compositional make-up.

The link between Gabrieli and Bach is not in the least far-fetched. The similarities are too many to be ignored. Both were devout, both were highly professional composers; both were progressives, mingling old-fashioned virtues with a surprising knowledge of the latest fashions. Both were intricate thinkers in music who found technical problems stimulating. Both were rediscovered in the 1820s and 1830s when the revival of 'old' music was being taken with great earnestness in Berlin. There were few Italians to champion their distinguished compatriot, no Gabrieli Society to match the Bach Gesellschaft, otherwise we might by now know his music more comprehensively. And if Gabrieli has not the sheer range of Bach, what he has to offer us is still very great. The late arrival of his music in our consciousness confirms a lesson of the Bach revival of the last century, which may not be displeasing to some: that the race, at least the long-distance race of posterity, does not always go to the swift—and the avant-garde.